EDGE
BOOKS

BLOODIEST BATTLES

D-DAY

THE BATTLE OF NORMANDY

BY ERIC FEIN

CONSULTANT:
Tim Solie
Adjunct Professor of History
Minnesota State University, Mankato

Capstone
press®
Mankato, Minnesota

Edge Books are published by Capstone Press,
151 Good Counsel Drive, P.O. Box 669, Mankato, Minnesota 56002.
www.capstonepress.com

Library of Congress Cataloging-in-Publication Data
Fein, Eric.
    D-Day : the battle of Normandy / by Eric Fein.
    p. cm. — (Edge books. Bloodiest battles)
    Includes bibliographical references and index.
    Summary: "Describes events before, during, and after the battle of
Normandy, including key players, weapons, and battle tactics" — Provided
by publisher.
    ISBN-13: 978-1-4296-2299-8 (hardcover)
    ISBN-10: 1-4296-2299-7 (hardcover)
    1. World War, 1939–1945 — Campaigns — France — Normandy —
Juvenile literature. I. Title.
D756.5.N6F45 2009
940.54'21421 — dc22   2008026556

Editorial Credits
Aaron Sautter, editor; Bob Lentz, set designer, Kim Brown,
    book designer/illustrator; Jo Miller, photo researcher

Photo Credits
AP Images, 7, 10, 17, 28
Corbis/Bettmann, cover (middle); dpa, 23
DEFENSEIMAGERY.MIL/War & Conflict, 9; NARA, cover (bottom)
Getty Images Inc./Time Life Pictures/US Coast Guard, cover (top);
    US Signal Corps, 14
The Image Works/Roger-Viollet, 15, 18
Mary Evans Picture Library, 6; Illustrated London News Ltd, 24
Newscom/Getty Images/Keystone, 16, 20–21; Getty Images/Three Lions, 4

1 2 3 4 5 6 14 13 12 11 10 09

☒ TABLE OF CONTENTS

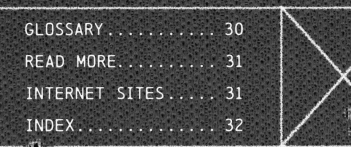

CHAPTER 1

FIGHTING TO SAVE EUROPE

The D-Day invasion of Normandy, France, was one of the most important battles of World War II.

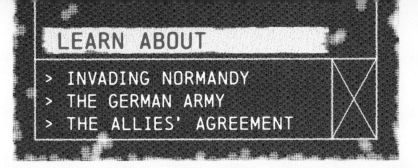
Early in the morning on June 6, 1944, one of history's greatest battles began. Led by the United States, Allied forces parachuted into France. The **paratroopers** were the first wave of nearly 175,000 Allied soldiers sent to France that day. This daring 24-hour invasion is known as D-Day. The fighting that followed was one of the most important battles of World War II (1939–1945). This battle is now known as the Battle of Normandy.

In 1944, the Axis powers controlled most of Europe. The Axis powers were led by Germany. Other Axis countries included Italy, Japan, and Romania. The D-Day attack at Normandy was the Allies' launching point for invading Europe. The Allies planned to first free France from Axis control. They could then fight to free the rest of Europe. The Allied nations included the United States, Great Britain, the Soviet Union, and several other countries.

paratrooper — a soldier who is trained to jump into battle by parachute

Hitler's Army

Adolf Hitler, Germany's leader, wanted to control the world. The German Army was one of the strongest in the world. Beginning in 1939, Germany's forces began taking over neighboring countries. By 1944, Hitler's army had conquered most of Europe. But Hitler's forces soon began showing signs of weakness.

Adolf Hitler built one of the strongest armies the world has ever seen.

Earlier in the war, German troops had suffered huge losses in the Soviet Union and Africa. By the time of the D-Day invasion, millions of German soldiers were dead or taken prisoner. Hitler's forces were also spread too thin. Many German troops still fought in the Soviet Union and on several other fronts. The army couldn't respond well to new threats. The Allies knew Hitler couldn't afford another major defeat.

Stalin Demands Action

Early in the war, the Soviet Union had some success fighting Germany. However, it soon needed help from the Allies. Germany had first invaded the Soviet Union in 1941. Since then, millions of Soviet soldiers and **civilians** had been killed. In 1942, Soviet leader Joseph Stalin demanded that the Allies invade Europe. Stalin believed a large attack in Europe would force Hitler to pull his troops back. This would give the Soviet military a chance to regroup.

U.S. President Franklin D. Roosevelt and British Prime Minister Winston Churchill knew they had to act. They feared Stalin might try to make a deal with Hitler. If the Soviet Union was lost to Germany, Hitler would be unstoppable. He would have Soviet oil to power his tanks and planes. He could also force the Soviet people to fight for his army.

In 1943, Roosevelt, Churchill, and Stalin agreed to an invasion of Europe. The invasion was scheduled for the spring of 1944. This gave the Allies time to gather the equipment and train the soldiers they would need to succeed.

civilian — someone who is not in the military

Winston Churchill (left), Franklin D. Roosevelt (center), and Joseph Stalin (right) agreed to work together to defeat Hitler.

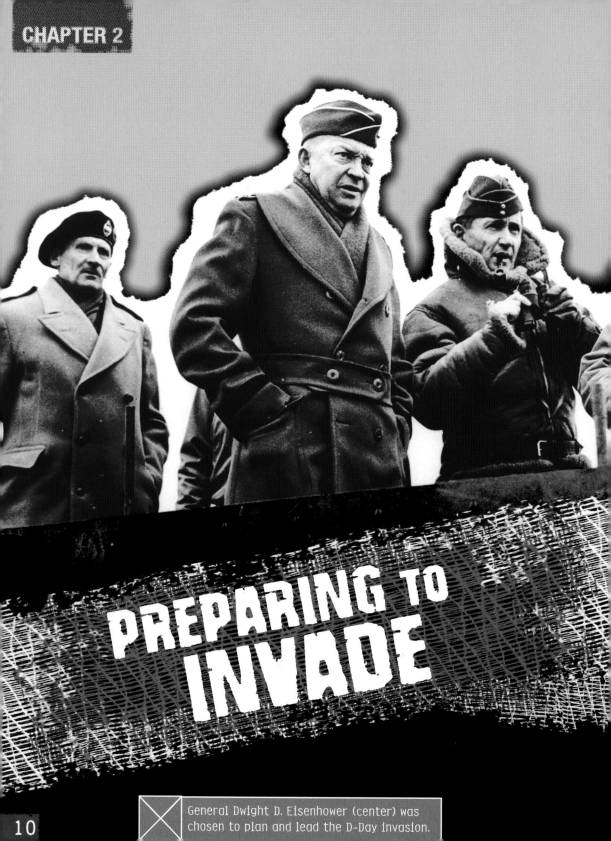

CHAPTER 2

PREPARING TO INVADE

General Dwight D. Eisenhower (center) was chosen to plan and lead the D-Day invasion.

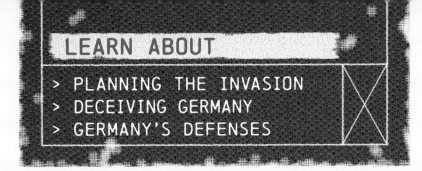
President Roosevelt selected General Dwight D. Eisenhower to lead the D-Day invasion. Eisenhower had been a successful commander in Africa and Italy. Eisenhower worked with other Allied commanders to plan the invasion. They named their plan Operation Overlord. The invasion had to be planned carefully. It would involve thousands of ships and planes. Tens of thousands of men would land on Europe's coast.

When to Invade?

Eisenhower first had to choose a time and place for the invasion. He chose to begin Operation Overlord in early June. The soldiers had to cross the **English Channel** to get to France. Good weather conditions were important. At this time of year, the weather would be calm enough for the ships to easily cross the channel.

English Channel — a narrow strip of the Atlantic Ocean between Great Britain and France

Where to Land?

Germany knew the Allies would try to invade Europe. Hitler had gathered Germany's forces on the northern coast of France at Pas-de-Calais. From there, it was only a short distance between England and France. The Germans thought it was the best place for the Allies to land.

However, Eisenhower knew Germany would be expecting an attack. He also knew Hitler had strengthened his forces at Pas-de-Calais. He chose to land far away on the beaches of Normandy instead. Normandy's beaches weren't ideal for landing large groups of men and vehicles. There were no ports for large ships to dock, and the tides were very strong.

The Germans didn't think Normandy was a likely place for an attack. They kept few men and weapons there. Eisenhower decided the Allies could surprise Germany by launching the invasion there.

IRELAN

FACT:

> **NORMANDY'S BEACHES**

The invasion took place at five beaches along France's Normandy coast. Each beach had a code name to keep the mission secret. The code names were Omaha, Utah, Sword, Juno, and Gold.

MAP

Operation Fortitude

The D-Day invasion required a huge amount of men and machines. To keep it secret, the Allies had to create a distraction. This plan was named Operation Fortitude.

Operation Fortitude involved creating fake military camps at Dover, England. To make the plan more believable, Eisenhower put General George Patton in charge. Patton had achieved many victories in battle against Germany. The Germans believed he was the best Allied commander. Having Patton at Dover convinced Germany that it would be the launching point of the invasion.

General George Patton (second from right) had great success against Germany in World War II.

Fake rubber tanks looked real when German spy planes saw them from the air.

The British and U.S. film industries also helped make Operation Fortitude believable. They made fake tanks and other vehicles out of rubber, plywood, and cardboard. When German spy planes saw them from a distance, the fake machines looked real. Meanwhile, thousands of real aircraft and tanks were gathered far from Dover.

Allied troops rode in Higgins boats to the beaches of Normandy.

Allied War Machines

The Allies had more than 12,000 planes and 5,000 ships ready for the D-Day invasion. Fighter planes like the P-51 Mustang were armed with several machine guns. Large bombers like the B-17 Flying Fortress carried thousands of pounds of bombs.

One of the most important vehicles was the Higgins boat. This transport boat had a flat bottom and a hinged front, or prow. The prow could be opened as it hit the beach. This design allowed soldiers and vehicles to quickly land on the beach. The boat could also back straight out to sea without having to turn around first.

Germany Prepares for Invasion

Germany's leaders didn't know where the Allies would land. But they knew an attack was coming. Hitler sent Field Marshal Erwin Rommel to France. Rommel's job was to improve Germany's Atlantic Wall. The Atlantic Wall was a system of defenses on the French coast. Rommel ordered millions of mines to be planted along France's coast. He also had miles of barbed wire strung across the beaches. The Germans placed sharpened poles in the sand to punch holes in the bottom of incoming boats. Above the beaches, they built concrete machine gun bunkers and trenches. They could then gun down Allied troops from the bunkers as they landed.

Field Marshal Erwin Rommel (front center) was responsible for strengthening Germany's defenses.

CHAPTER 3

D-DAY!

Thousands of paratroopers dropped behind the enemy lines in France before the main invasion.

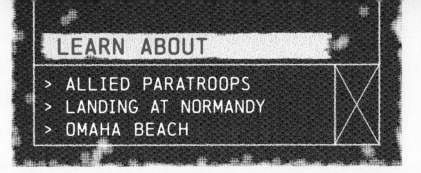

LEARN ABOUT

> ALLIED PARATROOPS
> LANDING AT NORMANDY
> OMAHA BEACH

On the evening of June 5, 1944, the Allied forces left for France. That night, more than 20,000 Allied paratroopers dropped into France. Their mission was to capture bridges, roads, and railways behind the front lines. This would stop German **reinforcements** from reaching Normandy.

Just before midnight, the paratrooper planes met German gunfire. Some were forced off course. They scattered many paratroopers away from their units. The separated paratroopers joined new units when they reached the ground.

Other paratroopers weren't as lucky. Their parachutes got caught on tree branches or church steeples. The Germans shot the soldiers as they struggled to free themselves.

reinforcements — extra troops sent into battle

The Allies used thousands of ships for the invasion of Normandy. It was the largest invasion fleet in history.

Hitting the Beaches

The main invasion of Normandy began at about 5:30 in the morning on June 6. The U.S. 1st, 4th, and 29th divisions were assigned to Utah and Omaha beaches. British and Canadian troops were to take Sword, Juno, and Gold beaches.

Within an hour, the first wave of soldiers hit the shore. The Higgins boats carried the soldiers to the beaches. The flat bottoms of the boats made the ride rough and bumpy. Many men were dizzy and seasick when they hit the shore.

When the Allied troops reached land, the Germans opened fire. Allied planes provided air cover for the land forces. They tried to destroy the German gun bunkers while the troops moved onto the beaches. But the planes couldn't take out all the German guns. Many Allied soldiers died before they even set foot on the shore. Many of the Allies' tanks and other vehicles were destroyed as well.

Death in the Sand

At Omaha beach, U.S. soldiers got a nasty surprise. The German guns were still working. The Allied planes had failed to destroy them. The American troops were shot at from every direction. The beach soon ran red with blood. The screams of wounded and dying men filled the air.

By midday, the U.S. Navy managed to knock out many of the German guns. This allowed U.S. troops to move the fighting inland. Meanwhile, British and Canadian forces succeeded in taking the other beaches. After securing a strong foothold, the rest of the Allied forces could now land safely.

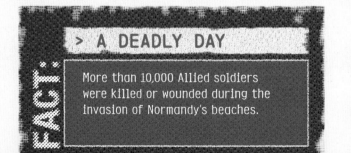

FACT:

> A DEADLY DAY

More than 10,000 Allied soldiers were killed or wounded during the invasion of Normandy's beaches.

The Germans gunned down many Allied soldiers as they landed on Normandy's beaches.

CHAPTER 4

AFTER THE INVASION

After taking control of Normandy, Allied troops began moving deeper into France.

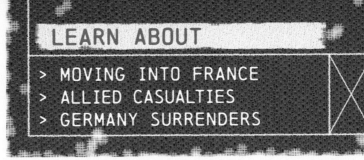
By June 27, there were about 1 million Allied troops in Normandy. The Allies' next goal was to move deeper into France and push back Germany's army. However, the Germans were able to slow the Allies' progress for more than a month.

In August, Eisenhower sent Patton and his Third Army into France. Patton's forces were well trained and efficient. Before long, they managed to reclaim large parts of France from the German Army.

On August 7, the Germans tried to strike back. They planned to take back the town of Avranches near the sea. But the Allies had discovered Germany's plans. Allied artillery and air strikes stopped the German tanks. Germany's forces couldn't break through the Allied lines.

FACT:

> K RATIONS

While on the battlefield, soldiers ate specially prepared food called K rations. A ration pack usually included dry biscuits, canned ham spread, a fruit-flavored drink packet, and a chocolate bar.

Freeing France

The Germans were finished in France. The Allies had taken about 200,000 German soldiers prisoner. About 240,000 other soldiers escaped back to Germany between August 16 and 19. But they left behind their tanks, artillery, and other military equipment. The Germans were in full retreat. The Battle of Normandy was over.

The Allied forces paid a heavy price to free France. They suffered more than 200,000 total **casualties**. Of those, more than 50,000 were killed in the fighting.

In spite of their losses, the Allies' success in Normandy was a major blow for Germany. For the first time, Germany was forced to retreat from western Europe. Hitler had to pull many of his forces out of the Soviet Union to strengthen his country's defenses. This allowed the Soviet Union to begin attacking from the east. Instead of conquering the world, Hitler found his country surrounded by the Allies.

casualty — a soldier who is missing, captured, injured, or killed in battle

 Many people celebrated the end of World War II with parades in Paris, France.

The War Ends

Although Hitler and his army were defeated in France, they refused to give up. The war in Europe dragged on. By the spring of 1945, Hitler realized there was no hope for victory. Many world leaders thought he would surrender. But on April 30, 1945, Hitler chose to kill himself. On May 7, 1945, the other German leaders surrendered to the Allies. Less than a year after D-Day, the fight to free Europe was finally over.

THE PLOT AGAINST HITLER

After losing Normandy, several German officers believed Hitler had lost control of the war. Field Marshal Erwin Rommel and others thought Hitler was leading Germany to ruin. On July 20, 1944, they tried to kill him. But they failed. Hitler suspected that Rommel was involved in the plot. At first, Rommel denied it. But he later killed himself to protect his family from Hitler. After Rommel's death, Hitler gave him a hero's funeral. Hitler didn't want to admit that one of his most trusted officers had tried to kill him.

GLOSSARY

artillery (ar-TI-luhr-ee) — cannons and other large guns used during battles

bunker (BUHNG-kuhr) — an underground shelter from bomb attacks and gunfire

casualty (KAZH-oo-uhl-tee) — a soldier who is missing, captured, injured, or killed in battle

civilian (si-VIL-yuhn) — a person who is not in the military

English Channel (ING-lish CHAN-uhl) — a narrow strip of the Atlantic Ocean that separates Great Britain and France

invade (in-VADE) — to send armed forces into another country in order to take it over

paratrooper (PA-ruh-troo-pur) — a soldier who is trained to jump into battle by parachute

reinforcements (ree-in-FORSS-muhnts) — extra troops sent into battle

surrender (suh-REN-dur) — to give up or admit defeat

trench (TRENCH) — a long, narrow ditch; soldiers fight in trenches during wars.

Hynson, Colin. *D-Day.* Days That Changed the World. Milwaukee: World Almanac Library, 2004.

Murray, Doug. *D-Day: The Liberation of Europe Begins.* Graphic Battles of World War II. New York: Rosen, 2008.

Platt, Richard. *D-Day Landings: The Story of the Allied Invasion.* DK Readers. New York: DK, 2004.

INTERNET SITES

FactHound offers a safe, fun way to find educator-approved Internet sites related to this book.

Here's what to do:
1. Visit www.facthound.com
2. Choose your grade level.
3. Begin your seach.

This book's ID number is 9781429622998.

FactHound will fetch the best sites for you!

INDEX